PUFFIN LITTLE

Little
Environmentalist

PUFFIN BOOKS

UK | USA | Canada | Ireland | Australia
India | New Zealand | South Africa | China

Penguin
Random House
Australia

Penguin Random House Australia is part of the Penguin Random House group of companies whose addresses can be found at global.penguinrandomhouse.com.

First published by Puffin Books, an imprint of Penguin Random House Australia Pty Ltd, in 2020

Other internal images: © kaktuzoid/Shutterstock.com, © Regina F. Silva/Shutterstock.com, © PinkPueblo/Shutterstock.com, © topform/Shutterstock.com, © TheBlackRhino/Shutterstock.com, © olllikeballoon/Shutterstock.com, © woraatep suppavas/Shutterstock.com, © olnik_y/Shutterstock.com, © StacyNineriver/Shutterstock.com, © Olga_Angelloz/Shutterstock.com, © GM art/Shutterstock.com, © Pogorelova Olga/Shutterstock.com, © Mallinka1/Shutterstock.com, © Tribalium/Shutterstock.com, © Oleksii.1994/Shutterstock.com, © Vasilinka/Shutterstock.com, © Lexi Claus/Shutterstock.com, © SpicyTruffel/Shutterstock.com, © N.Savranska/Shutterstock.com

Cover design by Ngaio Parr © Penguin Random House Australia Pty Ltd
Internal design © Penguin Random House Australia Pty Ltd

Printed in China

A catalogue record for this book is available from the National Library of Australia

ISBN 978 1 76 089701 7

Penguin Random House Australia uses papers that are natural and recyclable products, made from wood grown in sustainable forests. The logging and manufacture processes are expected to conform to the environmental regulations of the country of origin.

penguin.com.au

PUFFIN LITTLE

Composting

PUFFIN BOOKS

CONTENTS

HELLO, LITTLE ENVIRONMENTALISTS WELCOME TO MY GARDEN ...

You've caught me at a very exciting time.

I'm about to top up my **compost** bin
with the leftovers from my lunch.

The compost bin is the best place for food scraps like my sandwich crusts and banana skin.

If you don't know what compost is, don't worry!

As Little Environmentalists there are always lots of new and exciting things to discover about nature and the environment.

I'm going to tell you all you need to know about composting, and I'm going to show you how to make your very own compost.

We might be LITTLE, but we've got some **BIG** facts to learn.

Are you ready?

Then turn the page . . .

WHAT IS COMPOST?

Compost is a special kind of dirt that you can make by setting aside organic waste, like food scraps from the kitchen and dead leaves from the garden, and letting it rot.

This might seem like a silly, smelly idea but compost is great!

And here's why . . .

WHAT IS ORGANIC WASTE?

Organic waste is sometimes called green waste.

This waste includes any organic material such as food, garden and lawn clippings. It can also include animal and plant-based matter like paper, cardboard and wood.

Basically, organic waste is anything that was once living!

ORGANIC WASTE ONLY

Over time, all the leftovers and garden waste we've placed in the compost bin will **decompose** and turn into compost.

We can then use this spectacular soil in our gardens to grow flowers or vegetables or anything we want!

So how do we get from a load of stinky rubbish ...

to growing yummy vegetables and pretty plants?

To find out, we need to know a little bit more about **decomposition**.

DECOMPOSITION

When a plant or animal dies it will eventually be broken down into tiny pieces, and those pieces become part of the soil. This is called DECOMPOSITION.

Billions of tiny creatures help with this breakdown, including **worms**, **fungi** and **bacteria**. They are also called **decomposers**.

Decomposers use these bits of once-living things as their own food. These critters might sound like they have a pretty gross job, but it's a really important one. Decomposers turn those leftover parts of living things into compost. And compost is important because it's full of **nutrients**.

Decomposition doesn't just happen when we compost,
this cycle happens in nature every single day.

Have you ever been out for a walk in the park and seen
leaves and fruits on the ground that have fallen from trees?
After a while they get all brown and mushy,
and then, as if by magic, they seem to disappear!

But the leaves and fruits don't go away . . .

...They **decompose**. And all the good **nutrients** go back into the soil. This is the **cycle of decomposition**.

NUTRIENTS

Nutrients are the things that help

us grow and survive.

Your body uses nutrients from the food you eat to

build a healthy body. And plants need nutrients too!

They use nutrients to grow taller, sprout flowers and

make all of the plant parts that we eat as fruits and

vegetables.

All soil contains nutrients. When we mix our

homemade compost with the soil, we are adding even

more nutrients to help our plants grow.

The three main nutrients plants need are **nitrogen**,

phosphorus and **potassium**.

HOW DO PLANTS USE THESE NUTRIENTS?

NITROGEN

Plants use nitrogen for lots of things – from growing strong and healthy leaves to defending against pests.

Nitrogen is also what gives plants their green colour. If a plant is not absorbing enough nitrogen from the soil, the leaves of the plants start to go yellow.

PHOSPHORUS

Phosphorus is used by plants to help form new roots, make seeds and grow fruits and flowers.

POTASSIUM

Potassium helps make strong stems and stimulates fast growth. It's also used to combat pests and disease.

Okay, Little Environmentalists, now we know all about nature's **cycle of decomposition**, let's get back to my lunch scraps.

I've put my sandwich crusts and banana skin in my compost bin and mixed them up with lots of dead leaves from the garden. All I need to do now is sit back and let decomposition work its magic.

In a few weeks' time, when the compost is ready, I'll be left with a brown crumbly mixture, packed with nutrients, which I can use on my garden to grow more plants and vegetables.

This is the **compost cycle** . . .

THE COMPOST CYCLE

1. We eat yummy food, but sometimes we don't finish it all . . .

2. We **don't** throw our leftovers in the kitchen bin.

3. We throw them in the **compost bin!**

4. Our food scraps **decompose**, which creates compost.

5. The nutrient-rich compost mixed with soil helps plants grow.

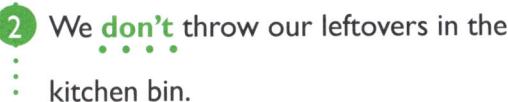

See, Little Environmentalists, compost is great!

WHY SHOULD WE COMPOST?

Compost is packed with wonderful nutrients and our plants love it! But there is another very important reason that we should compost . . .

We're going to learn all about how the LITTLE act of composting your leftovers has a **BIG** impact on the environment.

Understanding what happens to our rubbish when we throw it away is a good place to start.

WHERE DOES OUR RUBBISH GO?

Let's think back to my lunch scraps . . .

I had some crusts and a banana skin to throw away
and I put them straight in the compost bin.

I know exactly what will happen to them in there; they
will decompose and turn into nutrient-rich compost.

But what if I had decided to chuck my leftovers out with
lots of other bits of rubbish?

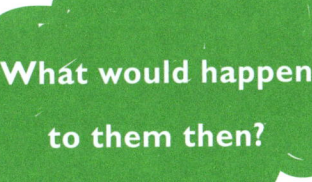

What would happen
to them then?

Would they still turn
into nutrient-rich
compost?

When we put our leftovers and food scraps in the general waste bin, they get mixed up with other types of rubbish.

This mixed-up mess gets taken away by a rubbish truck and dumped in a big hole in the ground.

This big hole is called **landfill**.

All the rubbish sent to landfill is buried, squashed together and then covered with more rubbish.

AEROBIC AND ANAEROBIC ENVIRONMENTS

When our leftovers end up in landfill they can't decompose like they would in the compost.

This is because the compost is an aerobic environment and landfill is an anaerobic environment.

An aerobic environment is a place with **LOTS** of oxygen. A healthy compost has lots of oxygen in it.

An anaerobic environment is a place with **NO** oxygen. In landfill, all the rubbish gets squashed together, resulting in there being very little oxygen.

We love an aerobic environment!

In the compost, all the oxygen-loving creepy crawlies, like the worms and bacteria, work their decomposition magic and break down our leftovers. They turn it into nutrient-rich compost.

But in landfill, the oxygen-loving creepy crawlies can't survive. In their place, landfill is swarming with **anaerobic** little beasties who tuck into our leftovers. Instead of turning them into lovely nutrient-rich compost, they produce two very nasty things called **leachate** and **methane**.

LEACHATE ——

These two things are bad news for our planet.

They affect our **air**, **soil** and **water**.

METHANE

LEACHATE

Leachate is a harmful, toxic sludge that is made when water and goo from food scraps mix with the other rubbish in the landfill.

Leachate can leak into groundwater and get into our rivers, harming the creatures that live there and dirtying the water that we drink and swim in.

METHANE

Methane is a powerful greenhouse gas.

The anaerobic little beasties in the landfill give off lots of methane when they break down all the squashed up rubbish.

GREENHOUSE GAS

Greenhouse gases are gases in the atmosphere (the air).

Methane is a greenhouse gas. There is another greenhouse gas you may have heard of ... **carbon dioxide**.

These gases act like an invisible blanket around our planet. They trap the heat from the sun and warm up the Earth.

This is called climate change (or global warming).

The problem is that greenhouse gases, like methane, are making the planet too hot.

Unfortunately, rising temperatures don't just mean we'll have a lovely long summer. The changing climate will make our weather more extreme and unpredictable. And hotter temperatures can lead to melting ice caps, rises in sea levels and animals losing their homes.

HELP!
THE ICE IS
MELTING!

So Little Environmentalists, now we know what happens when we don't put our food scraps in the compost bin, we can see how the **LITTLE** action of composting can have a **BIG** impact on our planet.

By composting our food scraps rather than sending them to landfill, we reduce both the amount of methane and leachate created and help to make our planet healthier.

Keeping food scraps out of landfill means we can follow nature's natural decomposition cycle. Food is grown, eaten and then the food scraps are composted back into the soil to grow more food.

That's another **BIG GREEN STAR** for composting!

A RECIPE FOR COMPOST

Did you know that composting is just like cooking? To make healthy, nutrient-rich compost we must follow a simple recipe.

All we need are **browns**, **greens**, **water** and **air**.

Not sure what some of these are? Don't worry, we're going to learn all about them in this chapter.

Okay, Little Environmentalists . . . Let's get cooking!

For decomposition to happen we need to make sure the mixture in the compost is just right.

The decomposers in the compost need a big scoop of **nitrogen-rich greens** and a handful of **carbon-rich browns** with generous amounts of air (oxygen) and a sprinkling of water.

The right amount of carbon and nitrogen makes the hungry decomposers very happy, and they grow fast. The faster they grow, the faster they will decompose everything into compost.

So what exactly are these **nitrogen-rich greens** and **carbon-rich browns**?

GREENS

Greens are quick to rot down and provide the decomposers with important nitrogen and moisture.

Apple cores, vegetable peels and tea bags, for instance, are called **greens**.

What other greens can you find around the house?

Perhaps some of these?

- **FRUIT AND VEGETABLE PEELS**
- **CITRUS RINDS**
- **COFFEE GROUNDS**
- **TEA LEAVES AND TEA BAGS**
- **PLANT TRIMMINGS**
- **GRASS CLIPPINGS**
- **FRESH LEAVES**
- **DEADHEADS FROM FLOWERS**
- **STALE BREAD**
- **CORN HUSKS**
- **BROCCOLI STALKS**
- **OLD HERBS AND SPICES**
- **EGGSHELLS**

BROWNS

Browns are things that rot more slowly. They provide carbon and make useful air pockets in the compost. This means the decomposers have plenty of air to breathe.

Egg cartons, cardboard and fallen leaves are called **browns**.

What other browns can you find around the house?

Perhaps some of these?

- PAPER TOWELS
- EGG CARTONS
- CARDBOARD TUBES
- SHREDDED NEWSPAPER
- SHREDDED OFFICE PAPER
- USED COFFEE FILTERS
- WOODCHIPS
- STRAW
- FALLEN LEAVES
- SMALL BRANCHES
- CHOPPED-UP TWIGS
- FALLEN BIRDS' NESTS

WATER

The decomposers that do the dirty work in the compost pile need **water** to survive.

For a perfect compost you will need just enough water for the compost to be moist, not wet.

Too much water won't do your compost any good, it will just make everything sloppy and slimy.

And if there is too little water the decomposers won't be able to survive.

So remember, Little Environmentalists, in dry months, you need to add water, and in wet months you need to protect the compost pile from the rain.

AIR

To make sure your compost has the perfect amount of air, you need to use a spade to mix up the pile. By moving the mixture about, you are adding air and shifting the less decomposed material on the edges to the middle of the pile.

If you don't mix up your compost every now and then, it will decompose very slowly and it might even turn into a slimy, stinky pile!

As well as water, the decomposers need air (oxygen) to survive . . .

Remember, we need an aerobic environment!

COMPOST NO-NOs!

As well as learning about all the things we **CAN** compost, it is also very important to learn about the things that **CANNOT** go in the compost. This might be because they don't rot, or because they are likely to attract rats or other vermin.

Here are some items that are big compost **NO-NOs!**

PLASTICS

☒

MEAT, BONES AND FISH

☒

PET POOP

☒

IN THE COMPOST

I like to think of my compost bin as a huge hotel for creepy crawlies. There are billions of **organisms** and **microorganisms** in our compost and each and every one of them help to decompose all the organic waste into nutrient-rich compost.

But do you know what actually happens inside the compost bin?

We've spoken a lot about **decomposers**, and now we are going to find out exactly **who** they are and **what** they get up to in the compost bin to transform all those greens and browns into super-soil.

ORGANISM

An organism is a living thing – animals and plants are organisms.

There are lots of **small organisms** that live in the compost and help with decomposition by producing **nutrients** like **nitrogen**, **phosphorus** and **potassium**.

Some small organisms you might find in the compost are: **mites**, **centipedes**, **slaters**, **ants**, **snails**, **beetles** and **earthworms**.

MICROORGANISM

Microorganisms are tiny living organisms that can only be seen under a microscope.

Microorganisms are everywhere – in soil, water, air, animals, plants, rocks and even the human body.

 Bacteria is a microorganism.

In composting, bacteria and other microorganisms break down organic matter and produce **carbon dioxide**, **water** and **heat**.

So who will we find checked-in at the Compost Hotel?

Look, Little Environmentalists! I've just spotted some new guests arriving at the Compost Hotel.

These **small organisms** are physical decomposers; they grind, tear and chew all the waste in the compost into smaller pieces.

WELCOME TO THE
COMPOST
HOTEL

Lots of earthworms seem to be checking-in. These wrigglers play a very important role in the compost. They are constantly tunnelling and feeding on dead plants and decaying insects, which they then poop out.

Their tunnelling also creates little pockets in the compost that enables water, nutrients and oxygen to filter down.

My poop is full of nutrients!

The earthworms and other mini-beasts break up all the big bits of waste into smaller chunks ready for the Compost Hotel VIPs – **BACTERIA**. And bacteria are responsible for most of the decomposition that happens in the compost bin.

Because bacteria are **microorganisms** we can't see them, but if we were to have a peek through a microscope we would find billions and billions of bacteria in the compost.

LET'S TAKE A LOOK

Compost bacteria are greedy and they eat almost anything! As the bacteria munches away on all the organic waste they find so delicious, they give off carbon dioxide and heat. This heat raises the temperature in the compost, which creates the perfect conditions for decomposition.

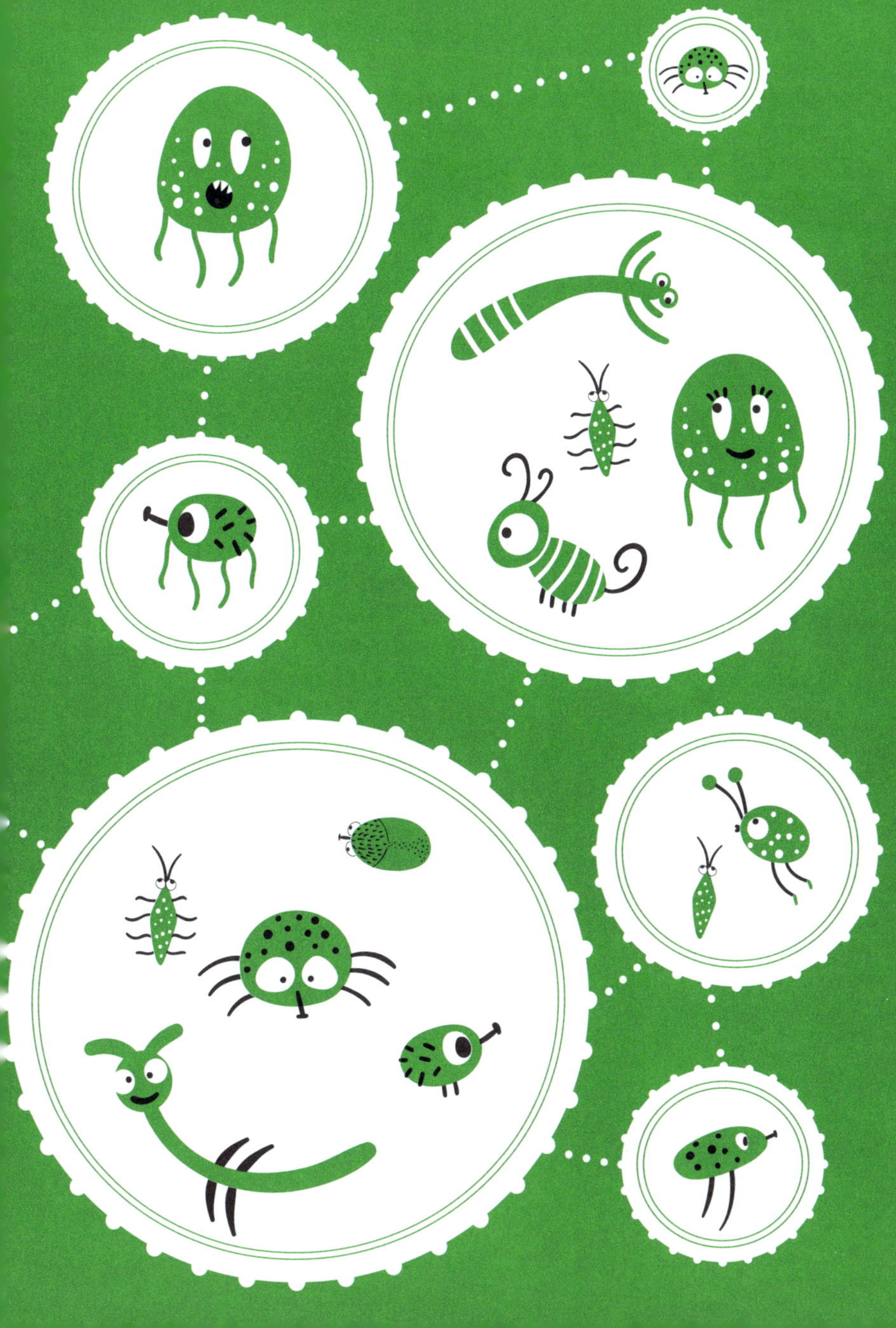

As soon as the bacteria check-in to the hotel they get straight to work, munching away, breaking everything down and giving off lots of heat as they go. In just a couple of days the compost can get as hot as 40°C!

The bacteria love the heat and over the next few weeks and months they continue snacking on all the scraps, breaking them down into smaller and smaller pieces. All this hard work raises the temperature in the compost higher and higher – it can get as hot as 65°C!

The bacteria do all their best decomposing work in the heat, but if it gets too hot, they won't be able to survive. This is why we need to mix up our compost every now and then, cooling things down and adding more scraps and much-needed oxygen to the compost (see **page 50**).

There are some other guests at the Compost Hotel that we haven't met yet – **FUNGI!**

There aren't as many of them as bacteria, but just like bacteria, they are **microorganisms** so we can't see them without a microscope.

In the compost, fungi work best in warm temperatures and are important because they break down all the tough rubbish that bacteria can't.

Compost is ready to use when all the hotel guests have done their job and everything has decomposed.

They will have turned all your greens and browns into a dark crumbly mixture with an earthy smell.

A lot goes on at the Compost Hotel!

It's very important to keep all the guests happy and comfortable. And it's up to us, Little Environmentalists, to look after our compost and make sure the guests have enough **food**, **air** and **water**, and that the temperature is just right.

If we don't, then it will take a very long time for decomposition to happen and things might get a little bit slimy and stinky.

COMPOST HOTEL CHECKLIST

☐ ## AIR:

Compost should be mixed daily or

every other day

☐ ## WATER:

Moist, not soaking wet

☐ ## FOOD:

Good mix of greens and browns

MAKE A LITTLE COMPOSTER

We've learnt lots of **BIG** facts about composting.

We know what it is, why it's good for the planet, what we can and can't compost and what all the creepy crawlies get up to in the compost bin.

Now is the time to put all this into action.

Scoop up your greens and browns, Little Environmentalists . . .

Let's make a LITTLE **COMPOSTER!**

You don't have to have a **BIG** compost pile to make compost.

A **Little Composter** does the job just as well, and what better place to start if you're a Little Environmentalist who is trying composting for the first time!

YOU WILL NEED

- **A plastic bin with a lid**
- **A Big Environmentalist to help drill holes in the bin**
- **Garden gloves**
- **Greens**
- **Browns**
- **Small shovel**
- **Watering can**
- **Compost thermometer**

If you don't have a garden and you are keeping your composter on a balcony, make sure you place a saucer underneath the bin to keep everything clean.

PREPARE THE BIN

To get started we need a plastic bin – not too small and not too big.

It is very important that your compost gets lots of air to help everything **decompose** faster. This is where you'll need some help from a Big Environmentalist . . .

They will have to drill holes in the bin.

The holes will need to be 2 to 5 centimetres apart, around the sides, the bottom and the lid of the plastic bin.

FIND A SPOT

Now you need to find the perfect place for your Little Composter . . .

Because this **composter** is nice and small, it will fit just about anywhere!

If you don't have a garden, it can be placed on a patio or balcony.

If you do have a garden, make sure you place your composter in a dry, partly shaded spot.

Anything you add to your composter should be chopped into pieces so that it will break down faster in the small space.

Greens, like food scraps, can be chopped small with a knife, or run through a blender to break them down. And any browns, like paper and cardboard, can be shredded to help spread moisture and air throughout the compost.

The secret to a healthy compost is to have the perfect balance of **GREENS** and **BROWNS**. For the best result make sure you add layers of browns and greens in equal amounts to your compost bin.

Don't make the layers too thick because this can clog up the mixture and slow down decomposition.

FILL YOUR COMPOST

LAYER ONE

Add your first **BROWN** layer to the compost bin. Use dry straw, twigs and sticks.

LAYER TWO

Add some more **BROWNS** – dry leaves.

LAYER THREE

Add a layer of

GREENS – fruit and

vegetable scraps or

plant clippings.

LAYER FOUR

Add a sprinkling of

water to moisten

these layers.

Continue layering until your composter is nearly full,

or you have run out of greens and browns.

TAKE CARE OF YOUR COMPOST

Once the small organisms and microorganisms get to work on the decomposition, it is up to you to take care of your compost.

Check in on it regularly, making sure all the guests at your Compost Hotel have everything they need for a comfortable stay.

Water your compost during the warmer months,

and make sure it doesn't get too wet in rainy weather.

WATER IT

Add fresh greens and browns and mix up your compost weekly. Your guests need lots of oxygen to survive.

CHECK THE TEMPERATURE

You don't want things to get above 90°C at the hotel. Regular temperature checks with your compost thermometer will let you know if you need to mix it up and add more greens or browns.

And then you wait . . . it's all about **patience**. But you must continue to check in and look after your compost.

If you find that your compost is not heating up, then you may need to **add more greens** to the compost. If you find that your compost is starting to smell, you may need to **add more browns**.

It won't be ready overnight, it can take weeks or even months. You will know your compost is ready to use when it turns a dark brown colour and smells nice and earthy. It should also be slightly moist and have a crumbly texture.

And here it is!

So Little Environmentalists,
what are you going
to do with your
nutrient-rich soil?

WHAT'S NEXT?

Now you have your wonderful, nutrient-rich compost, what can you do with it?

Do you plant directly in it? Do you fill your planters with it? Do you add it to the soil?

Turn the page for some LITTLE tips that will make a **BIG** difference to your garden.

FEED YOUR FLOWERBEDS

Help your new plants and flowers bloom by digging a 10 cm layer of compost into the soil before planting.

If your flowers have already been planted, simply spread a thin layer of compost around the base of the plants. Those all-important nutrients will work their way down to the roots and your plants will enjoy a healthy boost from all the goodness of the compost.

REVIVE YOUR POTS

Give your potted plants and containers an extra boost by removing the top few centimetres of existing soil and adding your freshly made compost.

Leave a gap around soft stemmed plants. This will provide food for your plants and flowers and is a great way to make them more healthy and robust.

But the most important thing,

Little Environmentalists, is to . . .

KEEP ON

COMPOSTING

Each year over half of our household rubbish is made up of food and garden waste. Most of this organic waste can be put in the compost bin.

By turning food scraps and organic garden waste into compost you can:

Keep your plants strong and healthy without using chemical fertilisers.

Reduce the amount of organic waste in landfill, preventing greenhouse gas emissions and leachate, which are bad for the planet.

Improve soil quality by adding rich nutrients into the soil.

GLOSSARY

AEROBIC: an aerobic environment is a place with lots of oxygen.

ANAEROBIC: an anaerobic environment is a place with no oxygen.

COMPOST: organic waste undergoing decomposition and used to fertilise land.

DECOMPOSITION: when plants or animals are broken down into tiny pieces and become part of the soil.

ENVIRONMENT: the interaction of all living things, the climate, weather and wilderness.

GREENHOUSE GAS: gases in the atmosphere that make the planet too hot.

LANDFILL: a big hole in the ground where rubbish is buried, squashed together and then covered with more rubbish.

LEACHATE: a harmful, toxic sludge.

METHANE: a powerful greenhouse gas.

MICROORGANISM: a microscopic organism.

NITROGEN: gives plants their green colour.

NUTRIENTS: help us grow and survive.

ORGANIC WASTE: includes any waste that was once living.

ORGANISM: a living thing, such as animals and plants.

PHOSPHORUS: plants use phosphorus to help form new roots, make seeds, fruits and flowers.

POTASSIUM: makes strong stems and helps with growth.

PUFFIN QUIZ

1. What is compost?

2. What **3 NUTRIENTS** do plants need?

3. Why is composting important for the environment?

4. Name **5 GREENS** that you can compost.

5. Name **5 BROWNS** that you can compost.

ANSWERS: 1. nutrient-rich soil 2. nitrogen, phosphorus and potassium 3. reduces the amount of methane and leachate in the atmosphere 4. might include: fruit and vegetable peels, tea leaves and tea bags, grass clippings, fresh leaves and stale bread 5. might include: paper towels, egg cartons, shredded newspaper, used coffee filters and fallen leaves.

A PUFFIN LITTLE BOOK